Cock

Mike Bartlett's plays include *My Child* (Royal Court Theatre, 2007); *Artefacts* (Bush Theatre/Nabokov/59E59, 2008), which won the Old Vic New Voices Award; *Contractions* (Royal Court Theatre, 2008); *Cock* (Royal Court Theatre, 2009); *Earthquakes in London* (National Theatre, 2010); *Love, Love, Love* (Paines Plough/Theatre Royal Plymouth, 2010) and *13* (National Theatre, 2011).

Work for radio includes *Love Contract* and *The Family Man* (both BBC Radio 4, 2007); *Not Talking* (BBC Radio 3, 2006), which won the Writers' Guild Tinniswood Award and Society of Author's Imison Award; *The Steps* and *Liam* (both BBC Radio 4, 2009). He directed D.C. Moore's monologue *Honest* in its first production by the Royal & Derngate Theatre, Northampton, in 2010. He is currently Writer-in-Residence at the National Theatre and Associate Playwright at Paines Plough.

Mike Bartlett

Cock

Methuen Drama

Methuen Drama

Methuen Drama, an imprint of Bloomsbury Publishing Plc

9 10 8

Methuen Drama
Bloomsbury Publishing Plc
50 Bedford Square
London WC1B 3DP
www.methuendrama.com

First published in 2009

Mike Bartlett has asserted his rights under the Copyright, Designs
and Patents Act 1988 to be identified as the author of this work

ISBN: 978 1 408 12743 8

A CIP catalogue record for this book is available from the British Library

Printed and bound in the United Kingdom

Available in the USA from Bloomsbury Academic & Professional,
175 Fifth Avenue/3rd Floor, New York, NY 10010.
www.BloomsburyAcademicUSA.com

Cock

For the Zona Rosa

Thanks to: Dominic Cooke, Jonny Donahoe, Elyse Dodgson, Ramin Gray, Clare Lizzimore, and especially Miriam Buether and James Macdonald.

Cock was first performed at the Royal Court Jerwood Theatre Upstairs, London, on 13 November 2009. The cast was as follows:

John	Ben Whishaw
M	Andrew Scott
W	Katherine Parkinson
F	Paul Jesson

Director   James Macdonald
Designer   Miriam Buether
Lighting   Peter Mumford
Sound   David McSeveney

Characters

John
M
W
F

The audience is raked down towards the actors.
There is no scenery, no props, no furniture and no mime.
Instead the focus is entirely on the drama of the scene.

Note

/ means the next speech begins at that point.

− means the next line interrupts.

. . . at the end of a speech means it trails off. On its own it
indicates a pressure, expectation or desire to speak.

A line with no full stop at the end of a speech indicates that
the next speech follows on immediately.

A speech with no written dialogue indicates a character
deliberately remaining silent.

A blank space between speeches in the dialogue indicates a
silence equal to the length of the space.

One

M	You take it out that's what you do you fucking take it out first otherwise what's the point?
John	Alright
M	It's not alright it's a fucking Don't. Don't you fucking dare, put it down first put it down.
John	I can't. I can't. Not when you're.
M	I'm
John	OH! Not when you're like that standing over me watching everything I do you're like a fucking. Pest. Is that the word? A fucking. Nuisance.
M	Nuisance?
John	Yeah look don't mock me, now you mock the way I speak, first you mock what I'm doing, what I'm making here, what I'm trying to do then you're mocking the way I speak.
M	You said it.
John	I know.
M	You spoke it
John	I don't need this. Not now. Not . . . do you understand?
M	Why am I being so nasty to you.

John	Why are you being so nasty to me . . . yes exactly why why why?
M	Because you're like a brother to me.
John	What?
M	You're like a brother.
John	You're playing now.
M	But you are.
John	I'm not your
M	No I know you're not. But that's what you're like, I'm mocking you like this, because that's what brothers do.
John	But you're not.
M	I'm not I know.
John	Fuck off now, go and watch your programme.
M	Why?
John	You're pestering me.
M	Pestering
John	If you don't just don't just I'll I'll
M	Look. All. I'm saying is. That you. Can't fucking cook. Can't fucking do anything with your hands.
John	Really?
M	Yes. Hands. No. Nothing. Nothing practical. Nothing that needs to be done. You're all gestures and waving. Cutting the air, and flapping them up and down all the time, trying to make a point, it's like EMPHASISING a WORD because you DON'T know how to use them and

	compensating with those fucking hands of yours have you seen them?
John	Have I seen my my hands?
M	They're like tennis rackets on the end of sticks. Like satellite dishes at the end of fishing rods. They're ridiculous.
John	Okay.
M	Ridiculous.
John	Okay.
M	I've missed you today.
John	Really.
M	Love you.
John	Right.
M	Really.
John	Right.
M	I'm like a puppy.

M	It took ten years off me. A shock like that.
	I know that's not what they say that's not the expression, but it did. I felt ten years younger after I picked myself up, and came to terms with the fact, with the fact I wasn't dead.
John	You felt glad to be alive.
M	I felt more alive. I felt like a fucking child again. I wanted to
John	Not dance.
M	Like run around and find someone and kiss them.

John	Who?
M	Someone. Doesn't –
	You know what I mean?
John	No.
M	You're not trying.
John	But you're alright.
M	I'm alright. Alright yes. Yes.
John	Because I was worried.
M	Of course.
John	When you didn't call.
M	Then when I did call.
John	When you did call yes, then I became even more worried breathing down the phone like that I don't want to be insensitive but you didn't think about me did you? Even for a minute. That I'd be worrying, I'd be dying thinking what might've happened, you didn't reassure me at all, the words you were using I thought you must have . . . I don't know concussion or something like that something that made you mad.
M	I didn't
John	You seem a bit
M	I'm not mad I'm not mad this isn't madness this is energy this is fireworks burning like on that one night of the year this is fingers up like sparklers this is eyes popping like fucking Roman candles this is the fucking bonfire in my

John	In your
M	In my I don't know my chest my arms my legs, my fucking hair I don't want to waste it, what what what? Why can't you go with me on this?
John	I think we're fundamentally different individuals you know that?
M	I don't
John	Fundamentally different people.
M	Are we.
John	I mean we live under the same roof, we go to bed at night we fuck and chat and cook and eat and everything but I think only now, only now I'm beginning to realise yes, look at us, that we're fundamentally different people. We're like. I mean you're eggs and I'm
M	Cheese
John	No what's the opposite? I don't know, I mean all the things we do they cover up the very basic fact that when it comes down to it, if you see something I don't know, dangerous, like a man with a knife, in the street, you know suddenly he's there, and you'll take a step towards him.
M	Yes.
John	But I'll run away.
M	Yes.
John	So do you see what I mean it's like a fundamentally different thing? If I got hit by a car, I'd be in pieces literally probably

literally you'd have to go to the hospital and collect me bit by bit and put me back together I mean I'd be a mess I'd be liquid you'd have to freeze me, solidify me before I could do or say anything you know okay I'm being dramatic and romantic but you know I'd be a fucking a fucking.

M   I know.

John   But you get hit by a car hit by a car like that and you're . . . better.

M   Yes.

John   You're more alive, like you say, you're more . . . there.

M   Exactly.

John   And I think that reflects something fundamental about our relationship.

M   You do.

John   I do I do.

M   Which is?

John   There's a gap.

M   Between? What? Us?

John   It's not working. It's nearly over. We're both ignoring the fact that it's only a matter of time before we'll be

M   No.

John   On our own.

M   Don't say that.

John   Just did.

M   It's not true.

John	It is true because I just said it so there it is. It's out there, look there it is right there can you see it yes, there on the floor between us this thing I just said, not going away
M	This is all a bit.
John	This is, yes, all
M	For me. All a bit much a bit hyper today everything's going so fast. I mean yes I feel better yes I feel like I appreciate everything more and that includes you yes before you say anything against it yes it includes you but I need something. Oh God I'm spinning, yes I need something to hold on to.
John	Not me.
M	You yes.
John	Not me. It's over. Look. That thing I just said is there between us in the way.
M	It's not.
John	It's going to be in a week maybe it will be I can feel it. So we might as well – No no no no no no don't fucking. Stand over there by the fake dog. Stand over there where I can see you but there isn't any danger you might. No. There. There.
M	Here.
John	Yes.
M	I'm alright here?
John	For now.
M	I might fall over.

John	You won't.
M	An illustration. Showing me the distance between us.
John	If you like.
M	But you're not showing me the distance, you're creating it, you put me over here, put that thing there between us.
	And you're saying it means.
	It means we're now
	We're
John	Yes?
	Well?
	Finish what you were going to.
M	What?
John	Say.
	Finish what you were going to say.
M	You want to go.
John	Everything we say to each other we're sinking.
	You and me.
	I'm taking a lifeboat.

M	Teddy bears waiting for a train. Very English.
John	Right.
M	Why this?
John	It's . . .
	kitsch

M	It is that it is kitsch. You want to get back you want to get back with me, you make a big fuss, then you change your mind, and you want to get back so you bring me teddy bears.
John	A random gesture full of humour and irony intended to provoke mutual feelings of goodwill, and find the giver endearing.
M	Okay.
John	So? Do you? Am I?
M	You were –
John	Endearing I mean.
M	You were the one.
John	I know.
M	The one who
John	I KNOW
M	So what's with the fucking bears. This *offering.* What? You think I don't *want* you back.
John	You didn't
M	I didn't. What? Say? No of course I didn't fucking say a word, of course I didn't. You say your piece and walk out I'm not going to beg you I'm not going to lower myself to asking why or asking you to stay we've always said, haven't we, if you want to go if you need to go go. And there you went.
John	And now I'm back.
M	With your teddy bears' fucking embroidered . . . party. What is this, an apology?

John	I suppose
M	So what have you done?
John	Nothing just what you know I've done. Walk out on you, leave you, and stay away, and mess you around and now I want to
M	This is covering something.
John	No it's smoothing.
M	No, more than that this is covering something up. You want to simply come back you have a change of heart something like that you want to come back in the normal way you buy me a bottle of wine or something I like, you buy me something simple, but you've had a had a longer.
John	No come on.
M	A longer Thought Haven't you. What's he going to say? When I come back in through the door. How can I make it seem like it's normal. Distract him. But distract him from? From? How can I persuade myself I want him? I know!
John	No no no.
M	Teddy bears. Yes yes yes. Jesus.
John	Okay
M	Here it comes
John	Yes

M	Here it comes in the distance.
John	I I I
M	A revelation. Thirty seconds and counting. So? So?
John	I still whack off to you every night.
M	A true fucking worshipper standing in front of me. A true *disciple*, John, aren't you? You whack off, no, you *still* whack off so you *still*, you *still* you see that implies a despite. We're not there yet are we? You *still* whack off *despite* . . .
John	What?
M	Despite. You s*till* whack off *despite* . . .
John	Despite nothing.
M	What?
John	Nothing.
M	Take it away.
John	What?
M	The bears the bears the bears I don't want them.
John	I think I'm in love and I need help because she's mad.
M	Bang! There it is. Love? Mad? She?
John	You can see why I'm confused.

M	You want help.
John	I need some straightening out.
M	Sounds like you've already
John	Not a joke that wasn't a joke. I just mean I need to know what's going on, because this woman this woman is
M	You want your boyfriend's help with the *woman* you're sleeping with.
John	Because really you're the only person.

M	Fuck off you fucked up little off my fucking land you get out get out now get out now
John	You don't mean that I know you I know
M	I thought we were brothers.
John	You said that but I never understood.
M	That we would stick together, like glue like blood
John	Blood yes.
M	Yes
John	And that's what I'm asking. Yes. Together. No matter what.
M	Exactly.
John	And this is what.
M	Okay.
	Okay.
John	Thick or thin we said and this is thin.

M	Okay.
	Okay.
	Stand further away and we might stand a
	You look so different now.
John	Please please
M	A different person.
John	I'm not I'm really not.
M	Shush.
	So.
	Okay.
	Tell me about it.
John	A week.
M	Lay it all out.
John	I am.
	It was a week ago.

M	Thank you for the detail
John	I'm trying to be honest.

M   You're always trying John, always trying, but have you ever actually done a thing in your life. Stop following me!

John   I'm not, but if you loved me like you're supposed to you'd sit me down and we'd have a conversation

M   We've never sat down like we're supposed to, I'm sorry but we've never had a conversation like this sitting down.

John   Yes we . . . have we definitely . . .

M   Not like what you're saying, that's never been how we worked never, but of course you've started, of course, making up fictitious and highly optimistic myths about our wonderful relationship which has since passed, about how *fantastic* things *used to be* and I'm sorry to disillusion you so soon into our reconciliation but we were not happy all the time, we rarely spoke to each other without doing something else and we always John, we argued all the fucking time.

John   Well I don't want to argue.

M   You cheated on me

John   / Not cheated.

M   with a girl a woman a female a chick, / cow, bitch

John   Stop it I don't want −

M   Don't want. Trying not to. Fucking DO something you piece of fucking crap on the floor of a shit shit road. Explain yourself or something. You're small. You're a half-arse. You're a lame duck. You're a stream.

John	But –
M	Do you understand John? A STREAM.
John	I don't think that means anything.
M	I want a RIVER!
John	I . . .
M	What?
John	I . . .
M	Yes?
John	I was going to say something.
M	Yes?
John	I've forgotten.
M	Jesus.
John	I do do things I bought you the picture.
M	Yes you did and no, no is the answer by the way I don't find you endearing. Yes you did and no Well. Not for the things you think I do.
John	But there's got to be something about me something that isn't all like that, otherwise why are we still here, still talking, why do you let me back, why did you think of us like brothers, which by the way is a really fucking weird thing to say but I assume I hope you said it because you wanted to express our commitment to each other our closeness our love that was more than sex more than friends was more like

	unconditional this ideal love you normally only find in families based on the idea that whatever we did whatever we did
M	I suppose yes I suppose and you're holding me to it.
John	Only that, yes, this is whatever.
M	Big fucking whatever though isn't it? Pointing pointing.
John	No. No. I've remembered what I was going to say.
M	Oh glorious fanfare cymbals and drum roll here it comes.
John	You're not as good-looking as you think.
M	Right.
John	Right. Yes. That's.
	You're lucky to have me.
	Okay?
M	Right. Well you're probably right.
John	Hmm.
M	And finally some balls.
	Finally a *statement*.
	Now we stand a chance.

John	She must be obsessed.
M	I thought we said.
John	She's always there. There's nothing I can do nothing I can do this isn't my doing alright. She's just there. That's why I didn't

tell you before I knew you'd be like this
think it was me but

Maybe she's outside right now.

M	Little fancy woman isn't she?
John	Stop it.
M	Nice little bit of skirt you picked up you fucking *lad*.
John	Alright alright
M	Cuntmuncher.
John	Very funny.
M	Mingediving muffmining wanker.
John	STOP. IT.
M	What does she want?

John	She thinks I'm straight.
M	Well you are from what you told me from the *graphic detail* you went into sounds a bit a lot like to me that you if you see what I mean that you are in fact yes yes not gay not that not gay but
John	No I don't think I'm, no I know I'm not. I'm not straight otherwise how would we still be doing anything?
M	A supreme act of the will?
John	No no I like it I do as you know and I love you and I share everything with you in my head all the time, I still, I mean you give me a really big dick metaphorically or actually sometimes looking at you, or thinking of you coming home, or you know when I'm at work got your picture on my

desktop on my phone everywhere still now so no no.

I suppose I like both but that's okay isn't it that's okay?

M   That's okay John yes it's absolutely okay to like both

John   Yes. Exactly.

M   But not at the same time

John   Do you know what an apology is? Do you know what it means to accept one? That's what you did you accepted so the case is closed and we move on.

M   Oh we do I see how awfully.

John   Shut the fuck up. Bloody fucking fuck. That's you. I have a problem I have a really big problem, she'll embarrass me if I I don't know I have dinner with Mum and Dad and she comes over and starts talking or if she turns up at work and people ask questions.

M   So deal with it.

John   She's following me. Maybe she'll kill me.

M   A welcome gesture as far as I'm concerned I mean we mustn't forget John, we mustn't forget, you fucked and left her.

John   It wasn't just a fuck

M   This is what women do, what do you mean not just a fuck?

John   Well I want to be honest.

M   You liked each other.

John   Yes, at the time there was something.

M	Well maybe this is Disney, maybe this is high school the fucking musical and you're meant to be together for ever and ever John, maybe she's the one the one that you want yeah? The one you're looking for then no?
John	No.
M	OH!
John	What?
M	Oh, do you think?
John	What?
M	Do you think she's
John	What?
M	Would explain it.
John	No fuck off.
M	She might be.
John	She fucking is fucking not. You
M	Daddy
John	Cock.
M	Daddy.
John	Cock!
M	Daddy will you play with me?
John	How the fuck old are you you
M	Please Mummy why's Daddy doing that with that other man
John	If you don't close your fucking mouth before I even start counting to ten, I'll kick

you till your blood runs out till you fucking run out of blood.

M   All talk. You wouldn't kick you wouldn't do a thing. You'd try yes. You'd want to. You'd *intend* to like everything else but I'm safe because I know you John, and I'm sure your son will come to feel the same, nothing you want ever works out. You're fudge all over.

John   There is no son yes no baby

M   You seem so sure but you never mentioned a condom / in your statement

John   Well we did we –

M   And was she good-looking?

John   She's

M   A hot wet tight fuck?

John   Stop it.

M   Tall?

John   A bit.

M   Face?

John   Yeah.

M   Petite little thing that's what you like with girls is it?

John   No. No. It's finished it doesn't matter.

And she was tall, I said. No not petite, more like a man really.

M   What?

John   Quite manly I suppose.

M	Is that supposed to make me feel better? Soften the blow.
	That she was manly?
John	Yes.
M	You have no idea.
John	No.

M	I don't even believe that you would anyway. Is this a lie?
John	No.
M	I mean sexual feelings just don't work like that. Manly? What? Big hands? Shoulders? Penis?
John	Maybe it's all more complicated than anyone
M	Maybe for you it is. Yes, maybe you're the most complicated sexual being that ever existed. Because it doesn't seem to be the same level of problem for most people.
John	She was nice.
M	I can tell.
John	Yes.
M	And now she's following you.
John	Yes.
M	Lot of time on her big manly hands has she?
John	I don't

M	Is she unemployed?
John	Maybe.
M	Or Of course. She's retired.

John	I was sat there, sat there in that coffee shop telling her she had to leave me alone, and it turned out she wasn't following me, but it's just we see each other on the way to work, and and I felt it you know
M	Oh so fucking helpless.
John	Well, I know what you're implying with that but yes that's how it felt, that I had these feelings and at least I'm not hiding it from you and there was nothing I could do
M	Except fuck her.
John	Yes
M	Again.
John	Yes, back to her place and
M	What are you? Most people seem to come together pretty well, their atoms hold, and you can look at them and go oh, that's my mate Steve, that's the queen, but you, you don't seem to have grown coherently You're a collection of things that don't amount You're a sprawl A mob. You don't add up.
John	Kiss me

M	Why should I that's the one thing I have no intention, no reason to do absolutely no you've cheated on me twice and with a *woman* and I don't know if that's worse, and not just with a woman with some trannie
John	She isn't
M	With some tall manly strange thing if we're honest, we've uncovered this fetish of yours for Neanderthal women, and you've done it twice, you've put it in her considerable marshland more than once got exploring in the extensive rainforest she's got hidden down there, you've splashed it around and now you come back and you want me to kiss you.
John	Forgive me.
M	Forgive you? No No No No No.
John	Please.
	Thank you.
M	Always, unfortunately John, for me, always. And I hope you realise what that means. That means that I will always be this unhappy because I have a feeling that as long as we're together you will always do this to me, you will let me down, stand me up, cheat and lie and fail and cock things up like this, and then you'll wonder why I tease you why I'm always going at you, being sarcastic well it's the only way.
John	Then why are we

M	I don't know.
John	Well
M	But we are.
John	Yes.
M	I mean I'm not going anywhere.
John	Okay.
M	But you *have* to make a decision you prick.
John	Are you going to kiss me again?
M	What?
John	You looked like you were about to.
M	No.
John	Okay. Sorry. I just thought. Take your top off.
M	What?
John	For me.
M	Okay.

John	Thank you.
	And the rest.
M	Why?
John	Because I'm about to make a decision for you, in your favour, and I want to remind myself of what we have, that we are so close, and I want to look at all of you and remind myself that I love all of you even the fat bits, because I think that's the big difference between you and her – I'm I'm

	I'm fascinated by her and I mean I think she's just . . . wow! You know?
M	John why don't you tell your mum all this, she'll be pleased you've met a nice girl after all this time, well, I say girl.
John	Go on, take it off.
M	She always thought this was a phase and you've proved her right.
John	I think every inch of you is perfect.
	Right.
M	And?
John	I like that bit at your hip where the skin looks really tight. I'm going to touch it.
M	So this is a decision yes?
John	I love all of you.
M	Okay.
John	So
M	So decision made yes decision made?
John	Decision. Yes. Yes.
	I think Yes.
M	You think? For FUCK'S SAKE. No. No I think. I want some fucking commitment you You. Wet

Wet.
Fish.

John   Fish?

M   Maybe we should all meet up.
The three of us.
Finish it.
Yes, fish.
Fish, that's what you are.

John   Oh look.

M   Yes, well it doesn't mean anything.

John   Well.

M   This doesn't mean we're done about this.
It's not over.
I don't forget.
I'm like an elephant.

John   Like an elephant.
Yes.
Exactly what I was going to say.

Two

W	I think we live close to each other.
John	What? Sorry. Sorry I'm sorry.
W	I think we must live quite, sorry I hope you don't think this is scary but I see you often on the way to work, on the tube, then walking up towards the square. I recognise you, I think. Sorry – is that weird? But I thought I might as well say.
John	No, no of course you recognise certain faces, there's certain people you always see . . . there's this one guy I saw must've been a student and he used to wear a long black coat, white make-up you know like a goth?
W	Yeah yeah.
John	And I'd see him every morning and what he was wearing was like fuck you to the world you know? and course he looked a bit stupid but I loved the fact he didn't care.
W	Yeah.
John	I loved that, but then one day he got on the tube, and he was different, he'd had a haircut – and was wearing really normal, normal boring Topman clothes, everything about him had become like everyone else. I never noticed him again after that it was like he disappeared. Sorry that was a story wasn't it? You didn't ask for a story did you, just a oh look I recognise you, that's all you expected a kind of passing, and look I'm still talking. Sorry I'm a bit.

W	It's fine.
John	I'm a bit distracted.
W	Okay. It's fine. Okay. You're . . .
John	Yeah. Sorry.
W	Busy with . . . what? Work is it?
John	No no. Well yes, always, always busy with work but no
	I split up with, my relationship finished. Two weeks ago.
W	I'm sorry.
John	And I'm still . . . It's all I think about you know I expect you know what it's like.
W	You want to get back.
John	No. No it didn't work, it didn't work at all it was horrible, I mean it's like a, another world now, already like another time, but . . . you spend all that time sharing your life with someone else, and you don't miss them because they aren't physically there, you miss them because they're not in your head, when you watch a film you don't watch it with them any more, thinking of them, do you know what I mean? They've even left your own brain.
W	I was married when I was twenty-three.
John	Right.
W	Divorced after two years.
John	Yeah.
W	I was a kid really I don't know why I –

John	But you're not very – I know it's not polite but how old are you now?
W	Twenty-eight.
John	Right, really? Well Really? Twenty-eight? You look great.
W	Thanks.
John	Yeah yeah.

W	It's weekends that are the problem. Weeks are fine, they're great. Friday-night parties, after-work drinks this is when you're in your element, you can do what you want, but it gets to Saturday afternoon and if you haven't already planned to meet someone then you're there on your own and you know that right at that moment there's all these couples in the park, or going to Ikea you know? Sorting out the house. All these couples living the dream in their own world, doing things that couples do, doing the things they think they should do, but no no sorry that's bitter I mean these couples want to set up home, you know, they're thinking of the future. They're trying out marriage. What would it be like, could we spend our whole lives together, and looking I'm going to be honest shit – Jesus I'm really talking here.
John	It's fine.
W	I mean I'm so jealous of the ones that I think are really in love. I mean there's that whole Bridget Jones thing of finding a man,

John   So you do get

W   At the weekends yes, on a Saturday
                        afternoon or the evenings if there's nothing
                        to do and your flat then seems very small
                        and you've nowhere to go.

but I'll never do that I've been married, I've
found a man, you know, but it didn't work
because it wasn't right, I'll never do it again
I would rather be on my own than do that
however fucking lonely I get. Ha!

John   So you do get

W   At the weekends yes, on a Saturday
                        afternoon or the evenings if there's nothing
                        to do and your flat then seems very small
                        and you've nowhere to go.

John   Yeah.

W   And you can't really meet up with friends I
                        mean you feel they're doing it for your
                        benefit. I'm not moaning here, you know
                        that you do know that I'm just talking.

John   Well I suppose I've got all that to – I mean I
                        agree it has to be completely right. I mean
                        he always made me feel like I used to be, as
                        I was when we met, and you know we met
                        when I was twenty-one, twenty-two really
                        young, and I was always the younger one
                        and he wanted me to stay like that and it's
                        only now that I've realised, I'm a completely
                        different person, and acting like that like
                        twenty-two was making me so depressed I
                        mean I just stopped talking, stopped having
                        any real any real confidence.

W   It's over now.

John   Yeah.

W   It's good.

John   Yeah.
                        I know.

W	Fuck 'em.
John	Huh. Yeah. Huh.

W	Would you consider sleeping with a woman?

John	I see.
W	Well?
John	That's
W	Yes.

John	I see.
W	It's just a question. Please. We're just talking.
John	That's why you
W	No.

John	I don't mind.
W	That's not *why*.

Some people might think you were scrawny but I think you're like a picture drawn with a pencil. I like it. You haven't been coloured in, you're all

Wire.

John	So what are you saying?
W	I have no idea.
John	It's crossed my mind.
W	I noticed.
John	But I mean we're . . .
	But we've only just met.
	Maybe we should.
W	Should?
John	Not.
W	Of course.

John	Ha ha ha ha you're serious. I like it. Do I? I don't know. Oh oops I'm scared. I gave it away I'm shit-scared of you what do I say now?
W	Yes?
John	I've never found women attractive.
W	I'm not women, I'm me.
John	I know I know that I feel that.
W	So
John	I've never really looked at women I find them a bit like water

	when you want beer. Or like a minimalist house with nothing in it. When you're someone who's really into stuff.
W	Are you really into stuff?
John	There's no
W	What?
John	Well.
W	Yes it's different. Shall I just fuck right off where I came from.
John	No no no don't fuck right off where you. Just
W	Just what just what then?
John	Just sit there and let me have a think of this all through.
W	Of course.
John	I miss him.
W	I'm sorry.
John	But maybe this is a way of
W	No. No. I don't want to be a way . . .
John	No no.
W	Not a way, not a function. Only if it's only about me. Me.
John	Of course.

I really want to but I really am I mean I really am scared.

But we could give it a go couldn't we, see what happens?

W   Whatever you want if it's too soon. I mean I really like you I want to play a long game I certainly don't want to rush you, but this feels

Important.

You know?

John   I certainly have biological feelings, things are happening without going into details when I look at you there's definitely something going on.

W   For me too. Without going into details.

John   That's good I

W   Gap on.

John   Gap on?

Gap. On?

W   Yeah like a

John   Yeah yeah I get it it's funny.

W   Huh.

John   Huh.

I

Shall we go then?

W   Yours or

John	I don't have a mine I mean mine is his, I'm on a sofa with with a friend so not mine we can't go there so
W	No problem.
John	So we can't go there.
W	No problem.

John	All my life I've only really looked at men. But this is. I mean actually now. Now I'm looking at it. It's
W	What?
John	It's quite nice.
W	Like a Travelodge you mean? Sounds like something you'd say about a hotel room quite nice.
John	No I mean it's got a shape. A sense to it.
W	You can touch it if you want, but, and you may find this difficult, when you're first starting – beginner's guide this isn't it? – but please try to be delicate.
John	I didn't think there'd be so much hair.
W	There isn't so much.
John	No I didn't mean it like –
W	You can imagine I'm a man down there if it would make you feel more
John	No. There's nothing, nothing like this on a
W	AAAHHH

John   Is that – was that a good aaahhh or a bad
                  one?

W   Good one I think it's just you're it's a bit, I
                  mean, what are you doing?

John   Don't really know.

W   No. Don't stop. Don't stop. Not saying it's
                  not –
                  It's only it's sort of odd. It's a little bit like
                  I'm a science experiment, you're seeing how
                  I respond to stimulae in different, when you
                  . . . oooo

John   So circles are

W   Circles are . . . yes. good.

John   And what about in

W   In?

John   Inside

W   Yes in might be good in a minute if you just
                  hang on for, or no, okay, if you do it now
                  that's fine.

John   I'm thinking all the time, though, you
                  should know this, I'm thinking, I'm worried
                  is there going to come a moment when I'm
                  missing his cock. You know that I'm going
                  to miss it like a world-class tennis player who
                  gets to the final but had broken the racket
                  he's always

W   AAAHHH

John   Always played always won with and he
                  doesn't miss it until that big game, that big
                  point, but at that moment, the moment of
                  pressure that's when he really

W	Okay. Okay. Shush now. How are you doing?
John	Hard at the moment. If that's what you mean.
W	Yes, this is good.
John	Seems to be. I do like you.
W	So take them off. I want to see it.
John	Okay.
W	Okay okay okay. Yes. Yes. Right. That's. That's really up Isn't it?
John	What you were expecting?
W	I mean you're getting into this aren't you?
John	Yeah. I really like you. I'm so happy, I was so worried that although that's what I thought that I really was into sexually, romantically everything I was worried that actually it was just wishful thinking that maybe I wanted the children and the house and the life and what I considered normality, and that was really what I – but it's not. It's something really simple. It's this. There it is, looking at it. It's simple. I just fucking fancy you so much.
W	Yeah. Look at it there. Just look at it. I won't touch it for a moment. I just want to appreciate it

Twitching like that.
Sort of
Throbbing
I just want to look at it.
Before it goes inside
It's good isn't it?

And alright.
What if
Maybe now.
I just touch the end.
The bit I know about.
Just with my little finger.
Nail.
Just a very light

John   Aaaaagh.

W   Yes. And it twitches when I do that.
Doesn't it?

John   Yeah.
Aaaaagh

W   It twitches. It wants to get inside.

John   Yes.

W   It wants to fuck me to bits.

John   I think it really does actually yes.

W   Well here it is.
It goes in here.
So.
In it goes
Do your worst.

Oh.

John   Oh.

W   Yes

Oh

John	Yes
W	OH!
	YES!

John	I don't know how to explain but the thing is you have to stop following me.
W	Sugar?
John	Don't call me
W	Do you want some sugar?
John	Right.
W	In your coffee?
John	I don't want this coffee I only said yes to try and normalise the situation.
W	You head is very square I never noticed that before.
John	Can you please listen. I know you might be mad.
W	Oh come on. *Mad*? The *situation*? Don't patronise me John. *Following* you? We have the same route to work, we always saw each other you messed me around thought we have something and you go back to him. I'm angry John, I'm really fucking angry. I'm not following you, we just can't stop looking at each other.
	I mean I think there's still something
	But you went back to him I hope you're happy.
	The problem is we can't stop looking.
	I think you are really really scared.

Something happened when we slept together
I could see what happened in your head that
night, what you let yourself think for a
moment that maybe it was okay, maybe it
was allowed, and as I said before I'm just
very honest and I have a feeling it's only a
matter of time before the things that've
been nudged out of place in your head find
a new a new pattern and you realise that,
John, you can do what you like. It's okay.

John   You think I still like you.

W   Because

John   I don't.

W   But if you did

John   I don't.

W   What would you

John   I'm gay

W   What would you

John   I wouldn't

W   You see you can't even bear the question let
                alone the answer, you're trapped with him,
                and what he thinks you are but I know John,
                I know there'll come a time in a bit when
                you'll need someone to catch you because
                when it hits your whole world will really go
                upside down, more than it did before.

John   I'm in a relationship now.

W   I know. You went back but you're
                pretending.

John   I love him.

W	Like that. You're accustomed. It's what you're used to, that's all.
John	Yes, I mean it's only ever been
W	And I'm something so different.
	And you're worried.
	But you can't stop looking.
John	You're very assured actually aren't you?
W	
John	I said you were manly.
W	Manly?
John	That's what I told him.
W	I'm not.
John	I know
W	I'm not manly.
John	I know but
W	Why did you tell him that?
John	He asked what you looked like.
W	Is that what you think?
John	I didn't mean – you're not. It's just
W	You meant, what? My back? Shoulders?

John	I only said it to show him. To soften the blow, it's stupid I know but when I'm with him I always start to say – I mean I don't think you're manly at all.
W	Right.
John	I just didn't want to hurt him. If he thought you were.
W	It would've been better if you'd laid it all out. The truth.
John	I know.
W	Because you're being a real wanker to both of us at the moment.
John	I still really like you.
W	I'm not following you.
John	I know.
W	You still notice me all the time on the platform on the tube, getting coffee.
John	You're very noticeable.
W	Thank you.
John	And it scares me that's true.
W	Yes.
John	Because if what you're saying is right that I'm in the wrong place with the wrong person doing the wrong things, and really it's us it's *us* that could have a happy life with all the things we talked about –

Then . . .

I mean I'm so scared you're right.

Because that's what I feel.

I feel that you're spot on.

W   So?
Sugar.
What are you going to do?

John

John   But whatever you can do.

W   You want me to look more manly.

John   No. I don't mean

W   Strap my tits down, grow a moustache?
What?

John   No, just not as feminine as you normally.

W   It's insulting.

John   I'm sorry I'm sorry, but if, when you come
round, he thinks I was lying on top of
everything else.

W   I haven't agreed to this, I haven't even taken
in what you're asking I can't work any of it
out, you're using all these words you're
throwing them all at me, and asking me to
put them together why can't you talk
properly.

John   I don't know, something to do with my brain

W   Got that right, something wrong with your
brain, he wants me to come to dinner . . .

John   He wants me to invite you so we can talk.

W   We?

John   Yes to talk and we can see what should

W   There's no we.

John   Well there is.

W   No there's us us two but there isn't a we a
               three people because I don't give a shit
               about him you see, I don't even know his
               name

John   It's

W   I don't want to know his name.

John   No.

W   Of course not. I only care about you. We
               spend every other day together have done
               for the last two weeks so where does he
               think you're going what does he think you're
               doing?

John   He thinks I'm coming here.

W   Then why doesn't he leave you?

John   Or why don't you leave me?

W

John

W   Because you told me you'd made a
               commitment a decision and now it's dinner
               with the boyfriend so maybe I should, yes,
               leave you, you complete fuckwit – oh I'm
               sorry John don't look like that but this time
               it's true you needed to be stronger, why
               didn't you say no, no Mr Boyfriend, that's a
               completely fucked-up idea I think we should
               just call it a day.

John	I think he wants to understand it and we've been together for a long time you know so I feel I owe him something?
W	He wants to understand it why?
John	He wants to fight for me.
W	Him and me we must both be stupid what is it about you?
John	My eyes. That's what people have always said, I've never had compliments about anything except my eyes I mean I don't think I'm very good-looking, but my eyes.
W	Yes you're right there is something about them.
John	You know I'd protect you, if anyone laid a finger on you ever I'd smash them I'd torture them, I promise no one's ever going to do anything bad to you, I mean it. Really. When it comes down to it I'll be there.
W	Yes. I do. I do know that of course I do I think that's the thing. It was never just the sex was it? And as I said I don't believe there's only one in life, I mean I don't believe that. But I think you might be it. For me. The one. That's why I'm still here.
John	So. In that case. Please.
W	But please don't mess me around why why why do you want me to

John   Because if he meets you then he might see
                   how in love we are and he might let me go.

W   Let you go.

                   Jesus.

                   Jesus.

                   This is.

                   Look.
                   Maybe we should think about.
                   We're just going round in circles.

                   Maybe I shouldn't see you again.

John   Maybe.

W   I mean maybe I'm wrong.
                   And you aren't the right person and I
                   should give up.
                   Because there's so much emotional crap that
                   orbits you, you collect it like space junk and
                   it's always flying around you, and I'm tired,
                   I'm tired of avoiding it all.
                   I can see it now.
                   Floating about, round your head as I'm
                   talking.
                   All this stuff.
                   So maybe we shouldn't see each other any
                   more.

John   Yes. Maybe that's best.

W   Yes yes

John   yes.

W

John

Three

M   Are you going to get it?

John   Maybe it would be better if you did. Maybe
                 it would be better if you did.
                 Show some willing.

M   I'm cooking and she's your guest, well I say
                 she I mean I'm assuming she is technically a
                 female even if she looks like Ray Winstone,
                 no it's your bit of fuckpuppetry John, you
                 open the door to it.

                 It's waiting.

                 Standing there – outside now

                 Knocking. Knock. Knock. What's there?
                 Does it have a name?

John   Don't call her 'it'.

M   I might I just might, I just can't control my
                 mouth, I'm on *edge* here John.
                 You know that. And I just can't I just can't

John   You invited her.

M   Well I really want to know who turned your
                 head.
                 Turned it right round like that girl from *The
                 Exorcist.*

                 When are you going to tell her?

John   Tell her?

M   *Tell her.*

John   Not before dinner.

M   Dessert then?

John	You said the whole point is that it won't be so bad if she knows who I'm with. But if I tell her straight away she'll turn round and leave so
M	But you are going to tell her.
John	Yes.
M	Aren't you you little bastard.
John	She'll think she'll have the wrong house if I don't go now.
M	I think tonight might be your last chance.
John	Right. Right.
M	You can see how much I care about this.
John	Of course.
M	My hand is shaking with anger and nerves and God knows *love* for you and I'm having to go through this because despite what you say I have the feeling that I'm about to lose you and here I am trying to cut the fucking potatoes and I can't because I'm shaking, and just now I cut my fucking finger because of you you prick.
John	I'm sorry. I'm sorry. I promise I'm going to tell her, I'm never going to just leave you I promise you that isn't what this is about.
M	Well if you fuck this up I'm walking out. My own fucking flat you can have it I'd rather give you three hundred thousand pounds' worth of flat than spend another moment waiting for you if you fuck this up.
John	Okay.
M	Now open the door before she punches a hole in it. I'm imagining a yeti that's what

I'm imagining I want you to know that, a
kind of big horrible creature like she's made
by Jim Henson and operated by two men
inside, deep voice, like she's something from
Labyrinth what's that thing that thing I'm
thinking of they had it on *Blue Peter*.

John   Please.

M   What's it called?

John   Ludo.

M   Yeah. Ludo. Ludo!

John

M   Go on then.

John   Right right.
Jesus.

Hi.

W   Hi.

John   Please. Yes. Come in. Yes. You look.

W   Okay.

John   You look really good.

W   I tried to look less feminine.

John   Right.

W   I failed.

John   I can see that.

W   It's difficult, I'm not going to shave my
head, and I tried on these horrible jeans but
whatever I did just looked stupid so in the
end I thought fuck you John, I'm going to

be proud of us, proud of you and look
feminine, look really feminine.

John   No it's perfect.
You're completely right.

I love it.

Not manly at all.

W   Right.

John   Don't you want to come in?

W   Not really

John   Right.

Can I take your coat?

W   Thanks. Is he?

John   He's in the kitchen.

W   He's cooking.

John   I said I would do it, but he wouldn't have it
he says I'm terrible at cooking.

W   I don't think you're terrible at cooking.

John   It's not a competition.

W   Not terrible. You're not

John   It's not a competition please please it
mustn't be that.

W   Then what is it really?

John   He just wants to talk I think.

W   How's he going to take it? I feel sorry for
him actually I mean this is

John   Do you want to come through?

W   The living room.

John	Yes.
W	Is it yours? The flat.
John	Ours.
W	Great.
John	Shall we sit down?
W	Aren't you going to introduce us?
John	Well . . . yes. Yes. Do you want a glass of wine?
W	Red or white?
John	Either, yes, which?
W	Whatever goes with the food, what are we eating?
John	I have no idea.
W	Okay.
John	I'll find out. Oh. Well.
	Oh.
M	Hello.
John	Here he is.
W	Hi.
M	Introductions.
John	Yes. This is
W	We've heard a lot about each other I'm sure.
M	You're not manly.
W	No.
M	He said you were manly.

W	He lied.
M	I can see that.
W	I'm
M	Very feminine yes yes, that's clear.
W	Tits and everything sorry.
M	Tits and hips and everything don't be sorry darling. Don't be sorry. I'm sure he doesn't mind. Well. Interesting fabrication John.

Manly. |
W	Yes.
M	An explanation?
John	No.
M	Right. Well I don't know what he told you about me but I can be pretty feminine too. Nice dress.
W	Thank you.
M	Glad you've made an effort. I did as well as you can see, but John seems to think this is an informal affair.
W	I don't think it really matters.
M	Are you not going to enter into this conversation John? I mean it's a really good one, I'm really *loving* it, don't you want to take part?
John	Look, she's only just got here.
M	And already it's awkward! Who'd have thought? Never mind. It's beef we're having beef so I would recommend red.

	I heard you through the walls can't say a word in private in this house, but that won't matter because tonight we're all going to be very open and honest. Aren't we?
W	I hope so
M	A full and frank discussion.
W	Red please.
M	Red it is.
W	Thank you.
M	I'll go and find a suitable bottle, I'm sure you have this, you have different bottles suited to different occasions, some for when really very important guests are here.
W	I'm happy with whatever.
M	Others for when guests are
	less important.
John	Can you stop being so fucking bitchy.
M	BUT THAT'S WHAT THIS IS. ISN'T IT? THE ULTIMATE BITCH FIGHT.
John	No. It doesn't have to be. You just wanted to meet her. That's what you said.
M	Can I just confess I don't know why either of us are even in this situation. I mean look at him. Look at that!
W	It's a nice jacket.
M	I wasn't pointing at his jacket sweetheart.

John	Why are you calling her that? When did you get so fucking
M	He's pathetic.
John	*Camp?*
W	Well I don't think he's pathetic at all.
M	You don't. Well. Right.
W	And neither do you really. You're trying to make yourself feel better but you don't need to be mean like this. I'm not mean. I appreciate him there's respect maybe that's what he went looking for.
M	Yeah but if you lived with him.
W	I don't play games.
M	But if you lived with him.
W	Yes I'd like to. I'd like to do that.
M	Red yes?
W	Whatever you think is *appropriate*.
John	I'm sorry.
W	Don't be.
John	You like my jacket?
W	What?
John	You said you liked it yes?
W	Yes.
John	And how do I look generally?
W	Fine.

John	No oh no don't say fine. It's not about fine, it's about better than fine, it's about being brilliant, being exciting. So
W	I think you're beautiful, very exciting John. I love your clothes. I love the bits of mess you have it's all very you it's a halo of disorganisation and I love it.
John	Thank you.
M	Red.
W	Thank you.
M	Shall we sit, dinner will be a little while.
W	Alright.
	Well.
M	Shall we play a game?
John	What?
M	Cards?
John	
M	Discuss the news?
John	No.
M	What then?
John	Talk.
M	About?
John	Get to know each other.
M	We don't like each other.

John	You might get on.
W	What do you do?
M	Builder.
W	Really?
M	No. Not really. You.
W	I'm a classroom assistant.
M	Not a proper job.
W	I like it.
M	But really you want to be . . .
W	I'm very happy.
M	But really.
W	Really.
M	But really.
W	Yes alright maybe retake my A levels, train to be a doctor, in an ideal world that's what I'd do. Okay.
M	What happened first time round?
W	
M	With your A levels.
W	
M	Tragedy

or stupidity? It's always one or the other.

Broken family, death of a parent, the child goes off the rails something like that, or alternatively they've always been a bit thick but no one's ever told them, and then they get their results and it's staring them in the face. D F E spells stupid. For them. So? Is that what happened? Stupid is it?

W   I didn't give a fuck.

M   You didn't give a fuck. Oh. You didn't give a. That's clever you didn't give a *fuck*. Oh.

W   I hated school so I got out, started my own business.

M   Doing what?

W   Tourist guides of the city.

M   Tourist guides of the fucking city but now you're a babysitter so

W   Teaching assistant.

M   Yeah but that's the same so it all fucked up did it?

W   Worked for ten years, then yes eventually it fell apart yes.

M   I'm in business.

W   Really?

John   Yes he is.

M   Broker.

W   Fulfilling?

M   Not the point is it 'fulfilling'?

W   But you're happy?

M   Generally yes. Happy? Yes. Yes I really like my job.

That bit was honest what I just said, John tells me I should point it out when I'm honest because it's so rare but yes, actually, thank you for asking I'm actually genuinely happy.

W Well that's good.

John Is it just me or does it feel like we're all waiting for something to happen?

M Why did you fuck him?

W I thought it would be good, I don't think that's the surprising bit, it's surprising I felt anything. It's surprising it turned into a relationship and that we're all here now.

M In my flat.

W In your very nice flat yes.

M Yes. Okay.

W Yes.

I think we have a lot in common.

M Well we certainly have one fucking thing in common.

I'll go and check on the food. But that's just an excuse to leave really.

Honesty again there.

John	Music?
W	No.
John	I'm sorry. This must be horrible.
W	I'm not going to let you go John.
John	Thank you.
W	But you could contribute a little more.

	You'll break that.
John	Sorry.
W	What is it?
John	I don't know it was on the side.
W	Is it yours?
John	I don't know what it is, I'm sorry I'm not speaking, I'm sorry, I know it's weird but I'm trying to work out how to handle this who to be because I'm two different people with the two of you when you're separate and now I'm in the middle and no one.
W	Be yourself.
John	But I have absolutely no idea who that is, everyone else seems to have a personality a character but I've never, I've never – I used to do voices, I remember this, and I don't think anyone can really understand it when I say it but I remember one moment when I couldn't think what was my own voice, I'd been doing high voices and northern voices and men's voices and

	impressions of the teachers and my dad, and people on the telly and everyone was laughing and I tried to go back to my own voice but I couldn't remember what it was.
W	Sit down. It's alright.
John	And I always stand in front of the mirror for ages, every day I never know what to wear, when I go shopping for clothes I bring him and he says it's up to you, what do you like, and I think I don't know I don't have a fucking clue just choose something that isn't too strange, that means I don't look like a fucking idiot.
W	I think you look lovely.
John	Thank you.
W	And it's simple. You just need to pick the right moment.
John	For . . .
W	To tell him.
John	Right.
W	Then you'll know exactly who you are.
John	Right . . . Yes
W	You are going to tell him aren't you?
John	Of course, otherwise you wouldn't have –
W	That's the only reason I'm here.
John	Exactly.
W	When?

John	Dessert?
W	Yes yes. Sorry.
	Yes.

John	Well?
M	What? What?
John	How is it?
M	It's ready.
John	Okay well shall we sit down then, shall we make a start because I doubt any of us want this to go on all night.
M	No, we'll wait.

John	For what?
M	We're expecting one more.

John	I'm sorry?
	I beg your sorry. We're expecting . . .
	This is private, you know what that means? Or is this something you're orchestrating something you're setting up is this a trick, or a trial or what? Is this a fucking shaming or an inquest? Who who who is it? Who is it?

M   It's my dad.

John   Your dad?

W   Ha

John   Your dad? Why?

M   He's been lonely since Mum died and he
                 doesn't get out much and I thought

John   COME ON!

M   Well I'm regretting it now if I'm honest I'm
                 regretting it now, but when I didn't know
                 what she was like when I thought she might
                 be a bruiser or eight feet tall you know you'd
                 painted this picture and I thought it might
                 be good to have some back-up. I thought
                 it'll be two against one, and I was talking to
                 Dad about it and he offered to come round.
                 Course now I've met her, of course I know I
                 didn't need to I mean no offence sweetheart
                 but I'm not threatened but anyway he's
                 invited now and he'll be here in a minute
                 and we just have to deal with it okay?

John   So he knows.

M   Yes.

John   He knows about all of it?

M   . . .

John   You told him.

M   I was *upset*.

John	I'm sorry I'm really sorry I'm sorry you're here for this, this is
W	It's okay. I can see that it might be intimidating the two of us, and there's only one of him, not that this is a fight, not that we're fighting for you, but no I can see why he's been invited.
John	You're a fuck-up.
M	I'm not the cause. I'm not the cause of any of this.
John	Maybe we shouldn't talk about it. When he gets here. Maybe we should just have dinner and talk about uncontroversial things like politics or religion or cricket he likes cricket doesn't he?
M	None of us know anything about cricket. Do we? Unless you . . .
W	No.
M	No. Exactly. We all hate cricket. We can at least agree about that and anyway. You think we could all sit here for an hour and *not* talk about it? He'll want to. He's raring to go, because he loves you too John, he thinks we're great together he's completely disappointed in you for this. When I told him it was on the phone and it's difficult to tell but I think he was really upset he said absolutely I absolutely want to come and back you up give John a piece of my mind that's what he said so I don't think there's any stopping him.
John	Well this is a farce now, that's what this has become. This was serious, now it's parents

and tarts and vicars and I think we should cancel I really think that we should

W   John. Calm down. I'm sure he's a reasonable man. We're all civilised.

John   He eats tinned food straight from the tin I don't know.

W   I eat tinned food straight from the tin I think more people do that than you would imagine.

John   Oh God oh God oh God this is the worst night of my life.

M   I might check on the beef again.

John   NO. You know the beef is *fine*, you're staying here and when he gets here you're opening the door he's your guest. Stay there.

W   John, come on. It's fine.

M   Yes. She's right. John. This is a bit of a fuck-up, the whole thing I mean, but nothing disastrous is going to happen. I mean we're not starving, there's no earthquake or flood, and there are a lot of people living in the Third World right now and they aren't moaning they aren't going uh uh uh what am I, I don't know, they're playing football and smiling some of them and trying to make their lives better so please please please you in your nice shirt, your angst all this moaning is offensive really it's horrible because there's nothing really, there's nothing truly important going on.

John   You've nearly been crying all night like there now you're nearly going now . . . see

	it does *matter* of course it does and for me, I mean if you really think about it tonight could change everything. I turn one way I have children and a normal family
M	Normal.
John	I turn the other way and I'll always be wondering if I made the right decision. Our whole lives turn on tonight.
W	I thought you'd made your decision John.
	John.
John	Well I I I
	Oh God.
M	Of course he hasn't made a fucking decision he says it in the moment he says he knows what he thinks but really I mean why do you think I invited my dad?
	You don't know him as well as I do. He's worse than you think. There's all sorts of things you'll come to realise.
W	Really?
John	Oh no. No.
	Please.

Oh of course wonderful, and there he is. Fuck. Go on then answer it. Let's get on with it. I might be cutting my wrists when you get back.

M	Dad.
F	Hell of a time getting here. Tubes. Tube tubes. Hello. How are you?
M	It's good to see you.
F	Is she here?
M	They're both through there.
F	Bought you some wine.
M	Thanks.
F	Red. Don't know if it's good. Hard to tell isn't it, but it cost over seven pounds and that's what they say isn't it? If you go over seven pounds you can't go wrong really.
M	Thanks Dad it's very considerate.
F	Come here.
M	I'm sorry I'm sorry. It's so difficult.
F	Come on.
M	I thought it was all set for. For ever but he's sat there, he's just sat there and I don't know any more I don't know if he cares.
F	Come on. We've got work to do haven't we? Haven't we? And I'm here. I'll always be here for you.
M	But you won't. Dad. Not in the end. That's the thing, you won't. You'll die. But I always thought when you did at least he'd always be . . .
F	Well you've got me tonight at least. Shall we go through? Yes? Alright then.
M	You're very understanding.

F	Well we can't let this go can we. This is what you want?
M	Yes.
F	Well then. Off we go. Into battle. Through here? Hello. I'm his father. Hello John.
John	Hi.
F	You must be the other woman.
W	I must be yes.
F	You're not manly.
W	No I'm not.
F	He said you were manly tall with big hands that's what he said.
W	A lie was told I'm afraid.
F	Not that it changes things.
W	No I agree I don't think it changes anything.
M	Dad brought a bottle of red.
John	Oh. Did you? Thank you. It's very kind. It's good to see you. I'm glad you're here.
F	You are?
John	Well, all views are.
F	Yes well I have my views
John	Yes I'm sure.
F	I have my views can I sit here?
John	Yes yes.

F	Good. What are you cooking?
M	Beef. I thought we'd sit outside actually.
	In fact, now we're all here, shall we go straight through? Just through the doors at the back. I mean it's a nice evening so . . . John will you show them? And I'll bring dinner through in a second.
John	Alright.
F	Fine.
	Through here?
John	Yes
F	Does it matter where I sit?
John	No anywhere anywhere you like.
F	Maybe you two should sit together?
W	I'll sit here.
F	
John	Alright.
F	So.
W	He's right. Golden isn't it? Like Spain or something. A really nice evening.
F	Well it's nice weather but I don't know if I'd go that far.
W	
F	

W

F

W   Look I think we should all be pleasant, I think that's better for everyone.

F   But this isn't *pleasant* at all, is it?

W   Even so, I do hate rudeness.

F   Really?

W   Whatever the situation, call me old-fashioned but I do prefer courtesy. Consideration. It's how we get things done in a civilised way. Don't you think?

F   Where did he find you?

W   Oh well. Didn't last long. Rudeness it is.

F   John?

W   He didn't *find* me, Jesus Christ, I thought you were supposed to be from the days people had respect or something.
He didn't find me anywhere, we just always used to see each other around then eventually we got talking. Then we had sex and we discovered all the time that there was something there.
That we were falling in love.
Is that a fair summing up John?

John   Yes. Yes. That's right.

W   And before you complain, no, he wasn't in a relationship at the time.

F   That's what he told you?

W   They had broken up, the relationship was over.

F   Well it isn't over now.

John	
F	John why don't you speak up for yourself?
John	I really don't know.
	Sorry.
F	That's the last apology I want to hear that won't get us anywhere. And I think in the end this will come down to something very simple.
	You're being selfish.
	I think you need to work out what you are.
	Fast.
	I think you need to work out what you are.
M	There.
W	Smells great.
F	He's a good cook.
M	There . . .
	And there . . .
	John do the wine.
	Do start straight away when I've.
John	Red for everyone?
M	Yes.
F	Yes.
W	Thank you.
F	Good. Good. You don't say grace do you?
M	I don't think anyone does these days. What do you . . . We never said grace Dad. We never.
F	Well I do now.
M	Oh.

F	Since your mother died I've become a bit different, I think it changes you when you're living on your own. Saw those children on the television in Bangladesh or wherever that flood was. You know and they don't have food or water to drink, so these days I tend to say grace, not because I believe in God but because it's good to remember how lucky we are.
W	I really agree with that.
F	You do?
W	Yes. I think that's absolutely right.
F	Don't try to flatter me.
W	I'm not. I think that's spot on.
F	Right
W	I've been on my own for a while too.
F	Have you.
W	Difficult sometimes isn't it?
F	What are you doing?
M	Dad, do you want all the veg.
F	What?
M	Veg?
F	Oh yes, thanks.
M	So are you going to say grace? Or . . .
F	No it's all been said now. And we have more important things to discuss really don't we? John.

John   Right.

M   Please start, please do start.

F   You need to work out what you are don't you?

                  That's at the heart of all this.

                  Yes?

                  Because it's certainly not his fault, and although I don't know her, and I'm sure she had some hand in it, some kind of temptation whatever it was, well, we mustn't blame her. It's not her responsibility at the end of the day it's yours. There will always be other people, as well you know, it comes down to your behaviour.

                  It's down to you.

                  When you came home with my son, and you said you loved each other, it took some getting used to of course, I mean I've never thought it was wrong but it's just not how you imagine your life turning out when you have an only child, of course you hope for grandchildren and not, you know you hope for biological grandchildren really, but we're well past that now, we've had years to get used to, no not get used to, appreciate how lucky we are that our son is happy. And when my wife died that was her greatest happiness. That our son had found someone he loved. You John. You.

John   Please please don't make me feel guilty I do know the situation I'm well aware of what's going on and how important it is.

F	Hear me out John.
W	Yes hear him out please please don't *answer* / anything.
F	The fact is that some of us like women and some like men and that's fine that's good in fact that's good, a good thing, but it seems to me that you've become confused. Yes? I don't know maybe you want children that's understandable, maybe you're having a crisis of confidence, maybe you think for some reason you want to be more . . . normal, in some way, but the thing is, and I want you to know this, is that I love you as you are. You love my son, and you're a wonderful person I think you'll both be happy for your whole lives. So I see this as a blip, is what I'm saying. I'm sorry love. You're a blip.
W	Love.
F	You've never been interested in women before. Said so yourself.
John	That's right never before but
F	Well then. So this is obviously about something else. You're subconsciously trying to prove something, and we won't blame you for that, but you have to understand it has consequences for the people involved. Yes I think of course we grow in our lives, we evolve to some extent, from one year to the next, but we can't deny that some things are *fundamental* some

things are genetic. Baldness, or height, or sexuality. It's built in. You don't choose. I mean if we don't accept that we're back to what, how it was when I was growing up, prosecution, prison, *cures*, yes? Before your time but not for me, I remember it, when they thought something had gone *wrong* with people and we don't believe that now, we don't believe that something goes wrong or really in the end you have a choice, we think it's simply down to the chemicals in your brain, they go one way you like girls, they go the other way you like men and so on. It's how you're born.
No?
This is right.
Yes?

M   Yes.

John   I don't know, I don't – maybe it's not a switch, one way or the other, maybe it's more like a stew, complicated things bubbling up –

W   Did you plan that speech?

John   God . . .

F   This is what we call conversation actually, it used to be popular.

W   No, because you didn't really seem to be thinking it, it was just coming out of your mouth. Your brain was elsewhere.

F   I don't know what you're talking about.

W   You kept looking at my breasts as you were talking there there you're doing it now.

John   The Romans.

M	What?
John	The Romans just loved whoever they liked didn't they? They didn't have any of this.
M	The Romans fucked kids John, I'm not sure they're our best examples.
F	Look /
M	They threw *slaves* to the *lions*.
F	I'm not easily offended.
John	What this feels like actually . . .
F	But I can't let this go, I'm not looking at your breasts sweetheart don't flatter yourself
W	What is it with sweetheart what year is this? / *Sweetheart?*
M	Does everyone like the beef?
John	Yes.
W	Yes it's very good.
F	If I wanted to look at your breasts maybe I would but no thank you.
W	Your eyes flicker towards my body all the time. Scanning me up and down. I don't think men realise how obvious it is. All through what you just said, your brain was elsewhere, you were thinking actually she's quite attractive thought she'd be a dog but things have changed now now she's actually quite hot actually maybe you're now imagining a situation tonight where John goes back to your son and I'm upset and need comforting and you walk me

	home one thing leads to another, doing me in the shower, up against the wall, the water over my naked body or something, / this is how your brain works, you're a man, it's fine.
F	I don't believe this. Quite obsessed some nymphomaniac / you've found
W	Nymphomaniac what a fucking pathetic fucking offensive sexist little fucking thing to say if you don't mind me pointing it out but anyway it's alright, there's no need to be defensive, it's not that I think a man of your age *shouldn't* be thinking about sex, I think it's very healthy, but maybe not when he's giving a lecture about being *faithful*. Don't pretend you're on some kind of fucking high ground when actually you're down here in the sexy fucking dirt with the rest of us looking at my tits.
F	I understand, you think you're being shocking / but I'm not naive you have to understand, I'm really not.
W	I mean I take it as a compliment actually. It's always nice to have attention.
F	Yes yes. / Alright.
W	I know you just care about your son.
F	Yes.
	That's right. I do.
W	Of course you do. But you see what I'm getting at. Glass house yes? And I have a question. Was your wife gay?
F	My wife is dead.

W	Obviously I meant when she was alive.
F	No. She wasn't gay.
W	You?
M	Look
F	Of course not.
W	Not secretly, looking at men in magazines
M	Please stop it. Now.
W	Or your father?
F	No.
M	John, tell her to stop.
W	How do you know he hasn't ever looked at a man? He could've done. Nothing wrong with it.
M	I think he would've mentioned it when I came out.
W	But your mum was alive then so
F	I'm not gay.
W	In that case, if it's genetic where's the gene? Because I can't see it.
F `	Of course in the past, I'm sure the gene was there, of course, but was repressed in some way, hidden, and that's a shame, that's not right. But luckily it's different now and we can be open about what we are, so, John.
John	I'm sorry.
F	You're telling us you're bisexual.
John	No.

F   It's alright, there's no judgement or –

John   No. I mean there's never been any other women so

F   What then?

John?

Who are you really?

It's alright.

Take your time.

Take your time.

M   I've had enough.

You've been sat there dribbling into this really nice food that I've prepared stirring it around and around and we've all been trying to ignore the scratching and the mumbling and all of that, and you obviously you would rather throw our whole lives away than make a decision, yes?

John

M   Right. So I've had enough. I'm making a decision for you.

I don't want you. Maybe I'll find someone else, I don't know, I don't think they'll be as right as you but I can see now that you're never going to be happy never in your life, so go on go away with her and fuck it all up without me.

F	Now / hang on . . .
M	I've lost. I'm the loser. Out on the floor. KO. I'm dead.
F	Just wait / . . . you're getting.
M	Off you go. Off you fucking *trot*. Now. Out Out. Out of my house please Go on.
John	
M	
John	Really?
M	Yes.
John	Really though?
M	
John	Alright.
W	No. I'm sorry.
M	What?
W	You can't *reject* him. That isn't fair. What am I supposed to do then?
F	I think you should stay out of this.
W	I think *you* should stay out of this. It has to be John's decision. You understand that don't you, really, you know it has to be down to him. Because if he leaves now if you make it for

him, you'll never know, and I'll never know, for sure.

M   Fuck.

W   Yes.

M   You're right

W   Yes.

M   Bitch.

W

M   You're right.

But unfortunately that means we're back to John.

F   Pass the wine.

M   There.

W   John?

John

W   What do you think?

It's up to you.

John please –

F   Let him think.

W   I am that's all he's been doing but I want him to know that just because I'm not crying like your son or because maybe I can't exactly articulate how I feel I am dying as well here.

F	He's well aware of your feelings I'm sure.
W	He's sinking.
F	Sinking?
W	Down down look at him quicksand the more he sits there and doesn't *do* anything he –
John	Look . . . I . . .
W	Fuck. Oh fuck I'm losing you
F	Mad. / Mad
W	Okay. John. I'm sorry. It's up to you.
John	
W	It's up to you.
	Shit.
	Okay
	Sorry.
John	No. I've.
M	Yes?
John	I love you. I really do but sex with her is . . . better you have to, to *know* that I enjoy it more.
	And we don't argue, she doesn't make me feel like I'm less than you, she makes me feel intelligent makes me think I can do

	things with how clever I am, win things, that I'm unusually clever and I've never felt that with you sorry but not in the same way do you understand that?
M	I understand / what you're saying yes.
John	You always make me feel like shit because you're so fucking insecure we've talked about that
M	We've talked about that yes we worked through exactly that / thing and I try
John	And we don't have any plans for the future, you and me, you don't like to speak about it, you close my mouth sew it shut whenever I mention it because you think we're tempting fate or whatever but it means we've never progressed. And bringing your dad here, I mean what a fuck-up.
F	I'm / family John so –
John	So much insecurity about
M	WE'VE TALKED ABOUT –
John	YOU WANTED ME TO SPEAK SO FUCKING LET ME SPEAK AND DON'T CRITICISE ME IF I GET MY WORDS WRONG. She's better she's better than you look at her, I don't want to be crude but her vagina is amazing I love touching it and looking at it and she reads the same novels as me and she cooks as well, maybe not like you not technically in the same league as you but it's not from recipes in the *Guardian*, it's proper, she's learnt it from her mum, it's not Posh

It's not
Flashy, but it's –

M   Her grass is fucking greener right now that's
/ all.

John   You want to know what I am okay okay I
don't know okay.

When I was at uni and I finally decided I'd
do it and *come out,* all these people hugged
me and were *proud* of me and said how brave
I was and suddenly people were touching
me and I was wearing different clothes and I
was part of a *scene,* even walking differently I
think and everyone said the real me was
emerging, that I'd been repressed, and so I
thought I must've done the right thing then,
but it didn't feel like that to me. I had to
make more of an effort than before, and yes
I fancied men, a lot a lot but I never got why
that changed anything other than who I
wanted to fuck. What did it matter? Gay
straight, words from the sixties made by our
parents, sound so *old,* only invented to get
rights, and we've got rights now so

M   *Some* rights, not enough and they're under
attack all the time and not properly
defended in this country / even without
people like you – how did we get on to this?

John   They're horrible horrible words what they
do how they stop you

M   / 'horrible words'

John   and I can see now I can see that it's about
who the person is. Not man or woman but
What they're like. What they do. Why didn't
anyone say? I thought I thought your
generation was all for that. Peace. Love. So

why are you telling me that *what* I sleep with is more important that *who* I sleep with?

F   You love my son. That's what's / important.

John   Why are you telling me I have to know *what I am*? It doesn't matter, I love him because he makes me toast in bed and he's scared of cling film. I love her because she makes me feel as old as I really am.

She's gentle.

You've never been that.

M   Gentle. No.

John   No.

No.

But then again.

Maybe you're right, you might be the devil but at least I know what I'm getting into.

M   Yeah not a decision all that though is it?

John   I seem to be holding her hand don't I?

M   If you say so.

Maybe you should both . . . go then. I . . .
I need to get dessert.

W   John. No.

F   I don't understand this.

John.

This isn't you.

You'll regret this.

I better check.

W   Come on. Let's go.

John

W   John?

John   I just want to be happy.

W   We will be.

John   Yes.

W   You told him, he knows now.

John   Yes oh, but but they're right everyone I've
ever looked at or had sex with or anything
has been a man so

W   / That doesn't matter

John   except you and you seem perfect but maybe I'm depressed ill

W   / No

John   or probably this is just madness some emotional problem as he said no one else has these issues so maybe I need to –

W   You love me.

John   some psychosis caused by a homophobic society or something.

W   John you're thinking everywhere.

John   Maybe they're right, it's what I'm born with, my genes, my my my nature, just men, just gay, clear and

W   This isn't good for you. This house, him, look at how you are right now, he makes you feel young and small and stupid and it's not about sexuality at all, in the end, it's what he does to you.

John   Yes.

W   So now's when you leave.

John   Thank you. Yes. Yes.

M   *So* the dessert was cheesecake here it is: cheesecake. I made your favourite John your favourite in all the world, a nice cheesecake I think it was going to be a tactic a final gesture in case things hadn't gone well a final bribe or flourish or something a really big cheesecake but too late now and am I not pathetic? I spent all my time on this and look at it big and goopy I feel so fucking stupid bringing it

out now, really really I do but Dad said I
should show it to you, show you what I did,
the effort all that. So there it is John. There's
your cheesecake, if you feel like staying with
me for a bit you could have some we could
share a piece if you like but you're going
with her aren't you so you should probably
fuck off now, and me and Dad'll eat it
instead. Bye.

W   John's made his decision.
               We're leaving. Both of us.

               Thanks for the evening.
               I'm sorry it's been so difficult.

John

M

W   John . . .

               John come on.

John   I'm supposed to make a decision what I am.

W   What?

John   What I am.

W   No, you don't have to,

John   Yes.

W   Why do you –

John   I'm tired.

W

John   I'm . . . Sorry.

               It's . . .

M

W

John   I can't.

W

M

F   Alright then.

                  I'll get your coat.

                  Here.

                  Here you are.

                  Your coat.

                  Your coat.

                  Here

                  Here

                  Put it on.

                  He's made his mind up.

                  We've had enough now.

                  All of us I think.

                  Here.

                  Oh!

M   Fuck! What the fuck are you –

W   You want me to go? / John?

M	Are you alright?
F	/ Yes
W	So I'll go for ever, and me wearing your shirt, in a hotel in Paris, walking around glimpses of what's between my legs,
M	/ Fuck
W	all of that and everything else in the future, all leaving, all going, me pregnant eating biscuits and then the hospital bed, everything you described to me, everything we imagined, you holding my hand, and Jack's born and grows up there he is, and later Katherine and later their kids all six of them, gathered together to see us, all of us around the table at Christmas see? We're all smiling and I'm still looking great even though we're old, and everything about us both is beautiful until we die together and happy, all of that is walking out the door and you'll be left with him. Just him.

And his fucking cake.

So last chance.

Good decision John. Well done.

Fuck you.

Shit.

Look at me. Before I go. Look at me.

Right.

Bye.

M   I'm sorry. I'm sorry she was –
F   It's alright.
It's alright now.
Isn't it?
We're fine.

M   Come here.
John No.
No.
Go away stand further away.
M   Well fuck you I thought I was the one you.
John This isn't what I want.
I just.
I think this is easier.

M   Okay.

F   Dinner was excellent.

M   Thank you.

F   Do you want me to stay tonight?

             Or shall I . . . ?

M   Yes. Stay. The sofa bed. In the spare room.
             You've done it before. You know where it is.

F   Yes.

             Maybe I'll leave you, go upstairs, sort myself
             out.

M   Okay.

F   Good.

             Love you both.

M   Thank you.

F   I mean it.

M   Huh.

             Thanks Dad.

             So.

             You can help me take these through.

             After seven years I wasn't just going to let
             you go.

             If you want children we can have children
             and Christmas and whatever all of that, we

can have that ourselves, you know we can
do anything you want we can.

Are you going to help?

John   No.

M   You see, there's your nature. Coming
through.
That's genetic
Laziness.
Right there.

John   Can you go away, go away back inside the
house and close the door and leave me out
here for the evening on my own please.

M   You've made a decision now.

You can't go back.

John   I KNOW.

I'm your fucking trophy.

M

Before you come in can you bring the
cushions and make sure the lights are off?

Yes?

John?

John?

You fucking prick I'll go I'll go but I just
need a yes from you.

Cushions and lights.

Yes?

One little word. One little word and I'll.

Come on say it.

Say it.

Yes.

Say it.

Say it.

Yes I'll bring them in when I come and
switch off the lights.

Yes.

Say it.

Say it.

Say it.

Say it.

Methuen Drama Modern Plays

include work by

Edward Albee
Jean Anouilh
John Arden
Margaretta D'Arcy
Peter Barnes
Sebastian Barry
Brendan Behan
Dermot Bolger
Edward Bond
Bertolt Brecht
Howard Brenton
Anthony Burgess
Simon Burke
Jim Cartwright
Caryl Churchill
Complicite
Noël Coward
Lucinda Coxon
Sarah Daniels
Nick Darke
Nick Dear
Shelagh Delaney
David Edgar
David Eldridge
Dario Fo
Michael Frayn
John Godber
Paul Godfrey
David Greig
John Guare
Peter Handke
David Harrower
Jonathan Harvey
Iain Heggie
Declan Hughes
Terry Johnson
Sarah Kane
Charlotte Keatley
Barrie Keeffe

Howard Korder
Robert Lepage
Doug Lucie
Martin McDonagh
John McGrath
Terrence McNally
David Mamet
Patrick Marber
Arthur Miller
Mtwa, Ngema & Simon
Tom Murphy
Phyllis Nagy
Peter Nichols
Sean O'Brien
Joseph O'Connor
Joe Orton
Louise Page
Joe Penhall
Luigi Pirandello
Stephen Poliakoff
Franca Rame
Mark Ravenhill
Philip Ridley
Reginald Rose
Willy Russell
Jean-Paul Sartre
Sam Shepard
Wole Soyinka
Simon Stephens
Shelagh Stephenson
Peter Straughan
C. P. Taylor
Theatre Workshop
Sue Townsend
Judy Upton
Timberlake Wertenbaker
Roy Williams
Snoo Wilson
Victoria Wood

Methuen Drama Modern Classics

Jean Anouilh *Antigone* • Brendan Behan *The Hostage* • Robert Bolt *A Man for All Seasons* • Edward Bond *Saved* • Bertolt Brecht *The Caucasian Chalk Circle* • *Fear and Misery in the Third Reich* • *The Good Person of Szechwan* • *Life of Galileo* • *The Messingkauf Dialogues* • *Mother Courage and Her Children* • *Mr Puntila and His Man Matti* • *The Resistible Rise of Arturo Ui* • *Rise and Fall of the City of Mahagonny* • *The Threepenny Opera* • Jim Cartwright *Road* • *Two & Bed* • Caryl Churchill *Serious Money* • *Top Girls* • Noël Coward *Blithe Spirit* • *Hay Fever* • *Present Laughter* • *Private Lives* • *The Vortex* • Shelagh Delaney *A Taste of Honey* • Dario Fo *Accidental Death of an Anarchist* • Michael Frayn *Copenhagen* • Lorraine Hansberry *A Raisin in the Sun* • Jonathan Harvey *Beautiful Thing* • David Mamet *Glengarry Glen Ross* • *Oleanna* • *Speed-the-Plow* • Patrick Marber *Closer* • *Dealer's Choice* • Arthur Miller *Broken Glass* • Percy Mtwa, Mbongeni Ngema, Barney Simon *Woza Albert!* • Joe Orton *Entertaining Mr Sloane* • *Loot* • *What the Butler Saw* • Mark Ravenhill *Shopping and F***ing* • Willy Russell *Blood Brothers* • *Educating Rita* • *Stags and Hens* • *Our Day Out* • Jean-Paul Sartre *Crime Passionnel* • Wole Soyinka • *Death and the King's Horseman* • Theatre Workshop *Oh, What a Lovely War* • Frank Wedekind • *Spring Awakening* • Timberlake Wertenbaker *Our Country's Good*

Methuen Drama Student Editions

Jean Anouilh *Antigone* • John Arden *Serjeant Musgrave's Dance*
Alan Ayckbourn *Confusions* • Aphra Behn *The Rover* • Edward Bond
Lear • *Saved* • Bertolt Brecht *The Caucasian Chalk Circle* • *Fear and
Misery in the Third Reich* • *The Good Person of Szechwan* • *Life of Galileo* •
Mother Courage and her Children • *The Resistible Rise of Arturo Ui* • *The
Threepenny Opera* • Anton Chekhov *The Cherry Orchard* • *The Seagull* •
Three Sisters • *Uncle Vanya* • Caryl Churchill *Serious Money* • *Top Girls*
• Shelagh Delaney *A Taste of Honey* • Euripides *Elektra* • *Medea* •
Dario Fo *Accidental Death of an Anarchist* • Michael Frayn *Copenhagen*
• John Galsworthy *Strife* • Nikolai Gogol *The Government Inspector* •
Robert Holman *Across Oka* • Henrik Ibsen *A Doll's House* • *Ghosts* •
Hedda Gabler • Charlotte Keatley *My Mother Said I Never Should* •
Bernard Kops *Dreams of Anne Frank* • Federico García Lorca *Blood
Wedding* • *Doña Rosita the Spinster* (bilingual edition) • *The House of
Bernarda Alba* • (bilingual edition) • *Yerma* (bilingual edition) • David
Mamet *Glengarry Glen Ross* • *Oleanna* • Patrick Marber *Closer* • John
Marston *Malcontent* • Martin McDonagh *The Lieutenant of Inishmore* •
Joe Orton *Loot* • Luigi Pirandello *Six Characters in Search of an Author*
• Mark Ravenhill *Shopping and F***ing* • Willy Russell *Blood Brothers*
• *Educating Rita* • Sophocles *Antigone* • *Oedipus the King* • Wole
Soyinka *Death and the King's Horseman* • Shelagh Stephenson *The
Memory of Water* • August Strindberg *Miss Julie* • J. M. Synge *The
Playboy of the Western World* • Theatre Workshop *Oh What a Lovely
War* Timberlake Wertenbaker *Our Country's Good* • Arnold Wesker
The Merchant • Oscar Wilde *The Importance of Being Earnest* •
Tennessee Williams *A Streetcar Named Desire* • *The Glass Menagerie*

Methuen Drama World Classics
include

Jean Anouilh (two volumes)
Brendan Behan
Aphra Behn
Bertolt Brecht (eight volumes)
Büchner
Bulgakov
Calderón
Čapek
Anton Chekhov
Noël Coward (eight volumes)
Feydeau (two volumes)
Eduardo De Filippo
Max Frisch
John Galsworthy
Gogol
Gorky (two volumes)
Harley Granville Barker
  (two volumes)
Victor Hugo
Henrik Ibsen (six volumes)
Jarry

Lorca (three volumes)
Marivaux
Mustapha Matura
David Mercer (two volumes)
Arthur Miller (six volumes)
Molière
Musset
Peter Nichols (two volumes)
Joe Orton
A. W. Pinero
Luigi Pirandello
Terence Rattigan
  (two volumes)
W. Somerset Maugham
  (two volumes)
August Strindberg
  (three volumes)
J. M. Synge
Ramón del Valle-Inclán
Frank Wedekind
Oscar Wilde

For a complete catalogue
of Methuen Drama titles
write to

Methuen Drama
Bloomsbury Publishing Plc
50 Bedford Square
London WC1B 3DP

or you can visit our website at:

www.methuendrama.com